Poetry for Students, Volume 30

Project Editor: Sara Constantakis Rights Acquisition and Management: Margaret Chamberlain-Gaston, Jackie Jones, Barb McNeil, Robyn Young Composition: Evi Abou-El-Seoud Manufacturing: Drew Kalasky

Imaging: John Watkins

Product Design: Pamela A. E. Galbreath, Jennifer Wahi Content Conversion: Civie Green, Katrina Coach Product Manager: Meggin Condino © 2009 Gale, Cengage Learning

For product information and technology assistance, contact us at **Gale Customer Support, 1-800-877-4253.**

For permission to use material from this text or product, submit all requests online at **www.cengage.com/permissions.**

Further permissions questions can be emailed to **permissionrequest@cengage.com** While every effort has been made to ensure the reliability of the information presented in this publication, Gale, a part of Cengage Learning, does not guarantee the accuracy of the data contained herein. Gale accepts no payment for listing; and inclusion in the publication of any organization, agency, institution, publication, service, or individual does not imply endorsement of the editors or publisher. Errors brought to the attention of the publisher and verified to the satisfaction of the publisher will be corrected in future editions.

Gale
27500 Drake Rd.
Farmington Hills, MI, 48331-3535

ISBN-13: 978-1-4144-2147-6
ISBN-10: 1-4144-2147-8
ISSN 1094-7019

This title is also available as an e-book.
ISBN-13: 978-1-4144-4951-7
ISBN-10: 1-4144-4951-8
Contact your Gale, a part of Cengage Learning sales
representative for ordering information.

Printed in the United States of America
1 2 3 4 5 6 7 13 12 11 10 09 08

The Peace of Wild Things

Wendell Berry 1968

Introduction

"The Peace of Wild Things" is a poem by American poet, novelist, essayist, farmer, and environmentalist Wendell Berry. It was first published in *Openings: Poems* (1968), one of Berry's early collections of poetry, and was reprinted in 1985 in Berry's *Collected Poems, 1957-1982*. Written in the first-person, "The Peace of Wild Things" describes how the speaker finds a solution to the anxieties he feels during a sleepless night by going outside to a quiet, peaceful place in nature, near a body of water. In the presence of wildlife, water, and stars, he feels restored to equanimity, his troubles dissolving in the great peace he experiences in nature. "The Peace of Wild Things" is typical of Berry's work as a whole in that it attempts to find a balance between humans and nature; it shows how the natural world can play a vital role in healing the troubled human spirit. The poem belongs in the great tradition of nature writing in American literature, as embodied in the work of such classic authors as Henry David Thoreau, Ralph Waldo Emerson, and John Muir, and modern writers such as Annie Dillard, Mary Oliver, Edward Abbey, Loren Eiseley, and many others.

Author Biography

Wendell Berry was born on August 5, 1934, in Henry County, Kentucky, the eldest son of John and Virginia Berry. His father was a tobacco farmer, and both sides of the family had lived and farmed in Henry County for over a hundred years.

Berry attended the University of Kentucky at Lexington, graduating with a bachelor of arts degree in English in 1956 and a master of arts in English in 1957. He married Tanya Amyx that same year. Berry then studied at Stanford University's creative writing program on a Wallace Stegner fellowship, and in 1960 published his first novel, *Nathan Coulter: A Novel*. It was set, like almost all of his later fiction, in the fictional Kentucky town of Port William.

A Guggenheim Foundation Fellowship enabled Berry to travel to Italy and France in 1961, and in 1962 he taught English at New York University's University College in the Bronx. In 1964, he began teaching creative writing at the University of Kentucky.

It was during the 1960s that Berry first made his mark as a poet, with his collections *The Broken Ground* (1964) and *Openings: Poems* (1968). The latter contained the poem "The Peace of Wild Things." He also wrote his first book of essays, *The Long-Legged House*, in 1969.

In 1964, Berry and his wife purchased a farm in Henry County, Kentucky, and a year later became farmers of tobacco, corn, and small grains. Berry remained a member of the faculty at the University of Kentucky until 1977, when he resigned so that he could spend more time on his farm.

He continued to publish poetry at a steady rate, his books including *Farming: A Handbook* (1970), *The Country of Marriage* (1973), *Clearing* (1977),*A Part* (1980), and *The Wheel* (1982). Many of these poems deal with the natural world and the place of humans in it, often touching on spiritual matters. Berry's *Collected Poems, 1957-1982* was published in 1985. His essay collections from this period include *A Continuous Harmony: Essays Cultural and Agricultural* (1972) and *The Unsettling of America: Culture and Agriculture* (1977).

In 1987, Berry returned to teaching at the University of Kentucky, continuing until 1993, when once more he retired to his farm.

His later publications include *Life Is a Miracle: An Essay against Modern Superstition* (2000), *That Distant Land: The Collected Stories of Wendell Berry* (2002), *The Art of the Commonplace: Agrarian Essays of Wendell Berry* (2002), *The Way of Ignorance* (2005), the novels *Hannah Coulter* (2004) and *Andy Catlett: Early Travels* (2006), and two collections of poetry, *Given: New Poems* (2005) and *Window Poems* (2007).

As of 2008, Berry has written twenty-nine

books or chapbooks of poems, twenty-seven nonfiction works, mostly essay collections, and fourteen works of fiction, including novels and short stories. He has received numerous awards, especially for his poetry. These include *Poetry* magazine's Vachel Lindsay Prize in 1962 and its Bess Hokin Prize in 1967, the Aiken-Taylor Award for Poetry from the *Sewanee Review* in 1994, and the T. S. Eliot Award from the Ingersoll Foundation in 1994.

Lines 1-5

"The Peace of Wild Things" begins with the poet, writing in first person, describing what he likes to do when his mind becomes agitated and he needs to calm down. He presents himself as a man who is concerned about the state of the world. He appears to have no hope that the condition of the world will improve, although he offers no details about his worries. Perhaps he has in mind war, poverty, and injustice, all the things that plague humanity and seem to continue despite the best efforts of well-intentioned people to end them. In line 2, the poet makes it clear how deep this worry in his mind is, since he will wake up at night if there is even the slightest of sounds and the worry will start again. In line 3 it becomes apparent that he fears for the future, not only for himself but also for his children. Perhaps he harbors the fear that there may be some cataclysm or other devastating event that would radically change human society for the worse. He feels a father's care for the future welfare of his children. But he does not merely lie in bed awake, worrying. He has a solution, not for the world's problems, but for his own peace of mind. As he explains in line 4, he gets out of bed in the dead of night and goes outside and heads for a tranquil place in nature, no doubt nearby and a place he has visited many times before. It must be a lake or a pond, and he is familiar with the bird life he finds there, such as the wood drake (a male wood duck) and the great heron, a wading bird. The poet lies down near the water and seems to identify with the wild life he is now close to; he is deeply conscious of the beauty of nature.

Media Adaptations

- Some of Berry's poems were set to music by David Ashley White and published as *The Peace of Wild Things: For Voice and Piano* by ECS Publishing in 2004.

- Contemporary composer Andy Vores set "The Peace of Wild Things" to music for voice and piano in his song cycle titled *The Rainy Summer*. First performed in 1990 by Richard Morrison and Patricia Thom and self-published in

Brookline, Massachusetts, it is available from Andy Vores, 202 Fuller Street #6, Brookline, MA 02446, andvor@aol.com.

Lines 6-11

In these lines the poet explains about how getting out into the natural world cures him of the agitation and worry that he had been experiencing as he lay awake at home. He feels at peace now, and this is because he is able to sense and share in the way animals and birds live. There is peacefulness in nature because the animal and bird kingdoms do not, unlike humans, have the capacity to worry about the future. An animal or bird is incapable of feeling the agitation that the poet felt in the opening lines of the poem, because it has no concept of the future; it cannot worry that the future might bring something bad, unlike humans, for whom such thoughts come all too easily. Animals and birds therefore do not experience life as a burden. In line 8, the poet comments on the tranquility of the scene; the water in the lake or pond is still. It is as if he has suddenly stepped into another world that is altogether more peaceful than the human world.

In the final three lines, the poet widens the scene. In the previous lines, he has appreciated the presence of the birds and of the water. Now he becomes aware of the stars shining above him. He does not say that he looks up at them; rather, he feels their presence too. He thinks of the fact that the stars are not visible during the day; they show themselves to humans only at night, so it is as if throughout the day they are waiting to show their light. He concludes with an observation about how he now feels. Although he knows the feeling is only temporary, he feels at peace and at rest, and this gives him a sense of freedom.

The Human World versus the Natural World

The poem contrasts the turbulence of the human world, and the workings of the human mind, with the peace of the natural world. Human life is chaotic and dangerous. People are unable to live at peace with one another, and the news always seems to be bad. The poem was published in 1968 when the Vietnam conflict was at its height, and in the United States, Senator Robert Kennedy and the Reverend Martin Luther King, Jr. were assassinated. It is perhaps not surprising that someone writing during those turbulent times should sink into despair regarding the human condition. The poet cannot separate himself from the larger fate of the world, which he fears may eventually touch him and his children personally. It is notable that he seems most worried about something that has not yet happened but may happen in the future, and this is why he cannot sleep at night, or is frequently awakened and immediately starts to worry. In this capacity to envision and worry about the future, something that does not in fact exist, human beings separate themselves from the natural world of which they remain a part, since no other living creature has the capacity to imagine the future, let alone worry about it.

Topics for Further Study

- Go to a local park or other place where you can be alone in nature. Take note of how you feel. Do you feel different from when you are at home or with others? In what sense? What sort of a change have you undergone by being in nature? Why do you think this happens? Write a short essay in which you describe the natural scene and then reflect on how it affects your thoughts and feelings.

- Read the poems "Come Into Animal Presence" by Denise Levertov and "Sleeping in the Forest" by Mary Oliver. Write an essay in which you compare and contrast these poems with "The Peace of Wild Things."

- Write a purely descriptive paper in which you describe an animal you are observing in nature. It could be a bird, a squirrel, a deer, or other animal. What does it look like? How does it move? What is its purpose, as you watch it?

- For many years Berry has written about environmental issues, protesting against the misuse of nature. Select an environmental issue in your own locality that has relevance for how humans are using, or abusing, nature. Give a class presentation in which you describe both sides of the issue and make some suggestions about how it might be resolved.

The poet is deeply aware of this dichotomy between the human and the natural world, and when he is besieged by his own human capacity for worry, foreboding, and despair, he knows what the solution is, albeit a temporary one. He must allow nature to work on him, to fill him with its own kind of peace as an antidote to the restlessness that has come to dominate his mind. In other words, although humans can separate themselves from nature due to the ceaseless activity of their minds, they also have the capacity to be one with it; they can allow nature, which is always present in the moment, to pour out a balm on the troubles that they invent for themselves concerning an imagined future (or, although this is not a feature of this poem, a regretted past that, like the future, does not exist). The movement of the poem is therefore from fear and agitation—characteristics of the human world—to the peace that exists in the natural world. The presence of the water, the birds, and the stars, to name only the three things explicitly mentioned in the poem, is enough to restore the poet to himself, to his right mind, at peace with the world in which he lives, free from the thoughts that otherwise trouble him.

The Paradox of Human Complexity

At the heart of the poem lies a paradox: the human mind, for all its intelligence and sophistication, and human civilization, for all its ingenuity and vast achievements, have not led human beings to self-mastery; they have not enabled humans to acquire the peace and contentment that would allow them to live without fear. The pursuit of happiness may lie behind a great deal of human endeavors, but the desired happiness is rarely attained for long, if at all. For example, in "The Peace of Wild Things" the poet's mind is so much on tenterhooks that the slightest thing awakens him from sleep and leaves him awash in a sea of worry. In contrast to this, the wild things in the poem—wild in the sense of growing and living uncultivated, in their natural state, outside the reach of human civilization—live in peace, driven only by instinct, which can never lead them to feel at odds with their environment or with the innate conditions of their being. The paradox is that humans, who have so much more capacity to control their world and that of other living creatures than do the animal, bird, or plant kingdoms, often end up feeling more powerless, more at the mercy of circumstances than those other, simpler creatures who have no power to argue with the laws that govern their existence. The poem uses this paradox to present its theme of the complex (human) world finding what it needs in the simple world (uncultivated nature).

Allusion

An allusion in a work of literature is a reference to another literary work. It can be a reference to a person, an event, or simply a phrase that occurs in another work. When the poet writes in line 8 about his awareness of the body of water that is nearby, he uses words that echo a well-known phrase in the Bible, from Psalm 23: "He leads me beside still waters." The pronoun "he" refers to God. The psalm presents God as a shepherd who "makes me lie down in green pastures," which is echoed in "The Peace of Wild Things," as the poet also lies down in nature. Allusions may simply give a wider frame of reference to the work in which they occur, or they may serve a more complex, ironic function, serving to contrast or otherwise distinguish between the way the common words or phrases are used in the two works. In "The Peace of Wild Things," although the Biblical allusion in the poem is clear, there is also a marked contrast. In the poem there is no benevolent God leading the poet on and giving him comfort and peace. The poet himself takes the initiative to go into the presence of nature, and it is nature itself, not an external God, that provides the feeling of peace.

Free Verse

The poem is written in free verse, an open form of poetry that does not rely on traditional elements of rhyme and meter. Line lengths and patterns of stress are irregular. In this poem, the line breaks are largely determined by the syntax, the arrangement of the words in a sentence. The poem consists of five sentences of varying length. The first sentence takes up the first five lines and after that the sentences become progressively shorter and simpler, in keeping with the thematic movement from a complex to a more simple state of mind on the part of the poet. The varying positions of the periods that end each sentence create some variety in the spoken rhythm. The poem makes no use of rhyme except for the fact that the end of the first line rhymes with the end of the last line, which creates a sense of completion, rather like a piece of music that returns to the home key at the end.

Historical Context

Social Upheaval and War in the 1960s

It is not difficult to understand why someone writing in the late 1960s might express despair about the state of the world. For Americans, this period was fraught with social upheaval and the horror of war. In April 1968, the civil rights leader Martin Luther King, Jr. was assassinated in Memphis, Tennessee, where he had been campaigning on behalf of striking sanitation workers. In June of the same year, Senator Robert F. Kennedy was assassinated in Los Angeles after winning the California primary for the Democratic Party presidential nomination. In Vietnam, the Viet Cong, the forces of the communist North Vietnamese, launched the Tet Offensive in February 1968, attacking the South Vietnamese capital, Saigon, and other South Vietnamese cities. Although the Viet Cong suffered heavy casualties, the Tet Offensive showed that the United States, despite having nearly half a million troops in Vietnam, was not even close to winning the war. It was in the same year, 1968, that the My Lai massacre occurred, in which U.S. soldiers killed hundreds of Vietnamese civilians. The massacre was not reported until November 1969. In February 1968, Berry gave a speech to the Kentucky

Conference on the War and the Draft at the University of Kentucky in which he stated his opposition to the Vietnam War, "I see it as a symptom of a deadly illness of mankind—the illness of selfishness and pride and greed which, empowered by modern weapons and technology, now threatens to destroy the world" ("A Statement Against the War in Vietnam," in *The Long-Legged House*).

Elsewhere during these turbulent years, the Six-Day War was fought in 1967 in the Middle East, in which Israel defeated a coalition of Arab nations, and the Soviet Union, along with several Eastern European countries, invaded Czechoslovakia to crush the Prague Spring, an attempt by the Czech government to liberalize its communist society.

The Environmental Movement of the 1960s and 1970s

"The Peace of Wild Things" suggests the importance of living in harmony with nature. As a farmer and poet, Berry felt a deep connection to the land, and he also shared the concerns that were beginning to emerge during the 1960s about the degradation of the environment. The modern environmental movement is often traced to the publication in 1962 of *Silent Spring*, a best-selling book by Rachel Carson. Carson alerted readers to the dangers associated with the widespread use of pesticides. On his farm in Kentucky, Berry decided to practice organic farming, shunning the use of pesticides. In 1972, the U.S. government banned the use of the toxic chemical DDT, which had been widely used as an agricultural pesticide.

Compare & Contrast

- **1960s:** American nature writing flourishes. Edward Abbey (1927-89) writes *Desert Solitaire: A Season in the Wilderness* (1968) about the landscapes of southern Utah. Poet Mary Oliver publishes her first book of poetry, *No Voyage, and Other Poems* (1963). Denise Levertov (1932-97) publishes several volumes of poetry, including *O Taste and See: New Poems* (1964) and *The Sorrow Dance* (1967).

  Today: Prominent nature writers include essayist and novelist Barry Lopez, who publishes a collection of short stories, *Resistance*, in 2004; Native American poet and fiction writer Linda Hogan, who publishes *The Sweet Breathing of Plants: Women and the Green World* (2000) and *Rounding the Human Corners: Poems* (2008); and Rick Bass, who publishes his short story collection, *The Lives of Rocks* in 2007.

- **1960s:** In the Cuban Missile Crisis

of October 1962, the two superpowers, the United States and the Soviet Union, come close to starting a nuclear war.

Today: Although the cold war between the United States and the Soviet Union is over, the threat of nuclear proliferation remains. There is international concern over the possible development of nuclear weapons by nations such as Iran, a development widely seen as a threat to world peace.

- **1960s:** The modern environmental movement begins, and the federal government passes significant environmental legislation. The Wilderness Act of 1964 aims to protect nine million acres of federal land from development. The National Environmental Policy Act of 1969 aims to establish policies that enable humans and nature to live in harmony. The Act requires the federal government to produce an environmental impact study before taking any major action that affects the environment.

Today: The focus of much environmental activism is global warming. In 2005, the Kyoto Protocol, negotiated in 1997, comes into effect. In adopting this measure, countries commit to reducing the emissions—especially carbon dioxide—that contribute to global warming. As of 2008, 178 nations have ratified the Kyoto Protocol, not including the United States or China.

Elsewhere in Berry's home state, as well as in West Virginia, the seeds of new environmental problems were beginning to occur. In the late 1960s the coal mining industry began a practice known as mountaintop removal. The tops of mountains were blasted by explosives in order to gain access to the coal that was near the surface. This was cheaper than tunneling into the mountain to reach the coal, but it had negative environmental consequences. The dirt and rock removed was pushed down the mountain, filling streams and valleys, adversely affecting the habitats of a number of species. Berry was alert to all the damaging effects of this form of strip mining, and he published a fierce essay "The Landscaping of Hell: Strip-Mine Morality in East Kentucky," in *The Long-Legged House*, in which he condemned the practice, commenting, The land destroyed by strip mining is destroyed forever; it will never again be what it was…. Such destruction … makes man a parasite upon the source of his life; it implicates him in the death of the earth, the destruction of his meanings.

Berry called for the banning of strip mining by

state and federal governments. It was not until 1977 that Congress passed the Surface Mining Control and Reclamation Act (SMCRA) regulating the environmental effects of such coal mining, although environmentalists claimed that the law was ineffective.

The first national Earth Day was held in 1970, bringing environmental concerns to the attention of millions of people. The Environmental Protection Agency (EPA) was founded in the same year, and in 1973, Congress passed the Endangered Species Act to protect species and the ecosystems on which they depend.

Critical Overview

When Berry's 1968 collection of poems, *Openings*, in which "The Peace of Wild Things" appeared, was reprinted in paperback in 1981, Tom Simmons reviewed the book for the *Christian Science Monitor*. He comments, "While Berry's poems are neither intellectually scintillating nor complexly allusive, they shine with the gentle wisdom of a craftsman who has thought deeply about the paradoxical strangeness and wonder of his life." Although he does not mention "The Peace of Wild Things" by name, the following comment by Simmons might well apply to that poem: "The book includes meditations on the natural world which are essentially devotional in their ardent simplicity—yet which harbor no religious posing or affectation."

The publication of Berry's *Collected Poems, 1957-1982* in 1985, in which "The Peace of Wild Things" reappeared, produced more comment from reviewers. In *Library Journal*, Thom Tammaro states, "The interplay of the natural world and the human spirit is the informing principle in Berry's work," and Tammaro describes Berry as "a poet of rare compassion and grace, clarity and precision, reverence and lyricism." Writing for the *New York Times Book Review*, David Ray comments,

> [Berry's] straightforward search for a
> life connected to the soil, for
> marriage as sacrament and family

life, affirms a style that is resonant with the authentic. The lyricism is not forced, but clearly grows out of a deep bond with the earth and its generosity, with all of nature. He … can be said to have returned American poetry to a Wordsworthian clarity of purpose.

Among later scholars, Henry Taylor in *Southern Cultures*, although appreciative of Berry's overall achievement, states that there are

… occasional lines and sentences in Berry's poems that seem too ponderously overt with their messages, as if the poet had fallen into the momentary belief that assertively artistic use of language is, in some contexts, an irresponsible frivolity.

With this comment Taylor has "The Peace of Wild Things" in mind, and he identifies this poem as one of the less successful of Berry's poems. Taylor writes that "the plainness of the style has been taken so far in the direction of prose that the decision where to end lines is based on almost purely syntactical factors."

Such scholarly reservations aside, "The Peace of Wild Things" has proved to be one of Berry's most popular and widely read poems, appearing in anthologies and on numerous Web sites, posted there by ordinary readers who have enjoyed the poem and wish to share it.

What Do I Read Next?

- In addition to being a major poet, Berry is a prolific essayist. *Standing on Earth: Selected Essays* (1991), with an introduction by Brian Keble, is a representative collection of thirteen of Berry's essays from four of his earlier collections. The essays cover many topics, from poetry to farming and ecology.

- Poet Gary Snyder is often linked to Berry because of their common subject matter. *The Gary Snyder Reader: Prose, Poetry, and Translations* (2000) is a compilation, by Snyder himself, of his work, covering a period of forty-six years. The book includes not only Snyder's poetry but also his prose on topics such as the environment and Buddhism.

- Mary Oliver is a major contemporary poet whose work is characterized by close observation of the natural world and reflection on the relationship between humans and nature. Her *New and Selected Poems, Volume One* (2005) contains a representative sample of her work.

- In his meditative writings about nature, Berry is sometimes regarded as a modern Henry David Thoreau, the great American naturalist and transcendentalist writer. Thoreau's *Walden, or Life in the Woods*, first published in 1854, is his record of the years from 1845 to 1847, when he lived in a hut on the edge of Walden Pond, near Concord, Massachusetts. A modern edition was published by Beacon Press in 2004.

- *The Sacred Place: Witnessing the Holy in the Physical World* (1996), edited by W. Scott Olsen and Scott Cairns, is an anthology of poetry, fiction, and essays in which new and well-established writers present their encounters with the natural world and their reflections on the sense of the sacred in nature.

Sources

Angyal, Andrew, *Wendell Berry*, Twayne's United States Author Series, No. 654, Twayne Publishers, 1995, p. 118.

Berry, Wendell, *The Long-Legged House*, Harcourt, Brace & World, 1969, pp. 20, 66, 203, 205, 211, 212.

———, "The Peace of Wild Things," in *Collected Poems, 1957-1982*, North Point Press, 1985, p. 69.

Bly, Robert, *News of the Universe: Poems of Twofold Consciousness*, edited by Robert Bly, Sierra Club Books, 1980, pp. 3-4.

Burns, Shirley Stewart, *Bringing Down the Mountains: The Impact of Mountaintop Removal on Southern West Virginia Communities, 1970-2004*, West Virginia University Press, 2007.

Driskell, Leon V., "Wendell Berry," in the *Dictionary of Literary Biography*, Vol. 5, *American Poets Since World War II, First Series*, edited by Donald J. Greiner, Gale Research, 1980, pp. 62-66.

"Environmental Movement Timeline," http://www.ecotopia.org/ehof/timeline.html (accessed October 13, 2008) Gitlin, Todd, *The Sixties: Years of Hope, Days of Rage*, Bantam Books, 1987.

"Psalm 23," in *The Holy Bible*, revised standard edition, Oxford University Press, 1952, p. 585.

Ray, David, "Heroic, Mock-Heroic," in the *New York Times Book Review*, November 24, 1985, p. 28.

Simmons, Tom, "Poetry that Shines with Gentle Wisdom, Beauty," in the *Christian Science Monitor*, September 30, 1981, http://www.csmonitor.com/1981/0930/093002.html (accessed July 17, 2008).

Tammaro, Thom, Review of *Collected Poems, 1957-1982*, in *Library Journal*, Vol. 110, April 15, 1985, p. 76.

Taylor, Henry, "'All Goes Back to the Earth': The Poetry of Wendell Berry," in *Southern Cultures*, Vol. 7, No. 3, Fall 2001, p. 31.

United Nations Framework Convention on Climate Change, "Kyoto Protocol," http://unfccc.int/kyoto_protocol/items/2830.php (accessed October 13, 2008).

Further Reading

Bush, Harold K., Jr., "Hunting for Reasons to Hope: A Conversation with Wendell Berry," in *Christianity and Literature*, Vol. 56, No. 2, Winter 2007, pp. 214-34.

> In a wide-ranging discussion that took place on his farm in 2006, Berry talks about his poetry, the influences on his writing, and many other aspects of his life and work.

Goodrich, Janet, *The Unforeseen Self in the Works of Wendell Berry*, University of Missouri Press, 2001.

> Goodrich examines Berry's work in terms of his imaginative ability to turn autobiography into literature. She discusses this in terms of five different modes of being: autobiographer, poet, farmer, prophet, and neighbor.

Johnson, William C., "Tangible Mystery in the Poetry of Wendell Berry," in *Wendell Berry*, edited by Paul Merchant, Confluence Press, 1991, pp. 184-90.

> Johnson discusses Berry's poetry in terms of the presence of the sacred within the earth and the mysterious bond that unites humans with nature.

Kline, Benjamin, *First Along the River: A Brief History of the U.S. Environmental Movement*, 3rd ed., Rowman & Littlefield, 2007.

> This is a concise history of the environmental movement in the United States from the colonial era to the present. This edition has· been updated to include sections on the environmental challenges for the twenty-first century, including climate change.

Knott, John R., "Into the Woods with Wendell Berry," *Essays in Literature*, Vol. 23, No. 1, Spring 1996, pp. 124-40.

> This is an examination of the wilderness theme in Berry's work, which is a source of peace and joy that enables a person to understand and sustain his or her life.

Peters, Jason, editor, *Wendell Berry: Life and Work*, University Press of Kentucky, 2007.

> This collection of essays, reminiscences, and tributes to Berry covers the entire range of Berry'swork, including his poetry and his essays on sustainable agriculture and other environmental issues.

9 781375 392860